Going to Work SCHOOL EDITION · Going to Work SCHOOL EDITION · Going to Work SCHOOL EDITION · Going to
CHOOL EDITION · Going to Work SCHOOL EDITION · Going to Work SCHOOL EDITION · CHOOL ED
oing to Work SCHOOL EDITION · Going to Work SCHOOL EDITION · Going to
CHOOL EDITION · Going to Work SCHOOL EDITION · Going to Work SCHOOL EDITION · HOOL ED

Going To Work
SCHOOL EDITION

Nurses

Buddy BOOKS
Going To Work

ABDO
Publishing Company

A Buddy **Book by**
Julie Murray

VISIT US AT
www.abdopublishing.com

Published by ABDO Publishing Company, 8000 West 78th Street, Edina, Minnesota 55439.

Copyright © 2011 by Abdo Consulting Group, Inc. International copyrights reserved in all countries. No part of this book may be reproduced in any form without written permission from the publisher. Buddy Books™ is a trademark and logo of ABDO Publishing Company.

Printed in the United States of America, North Mankato, Minnesota.
022010
092010

 PRINTED ON RECYCLED PAPER

Coordinating Series Editor: Rochelle Baltzer
Editor: Sarah Tieck
Contributing Editors: Heidi M.D. Elston, Megan M. Gunderson, BreAnn Rumsch, Marcia Zappa
Graphic Design: Maria Hosley
Cover Photograph: *AP Photo*: Mickey Welsh/Montgomery Advertiser.
Interior Photographs/Illustrations: *AP Photo*: Emily Behlmann/Garden City Telegram (p. 9), Jeff Gentner (p. 11), Samuel Hoffman/The Fort Wayne Journal Gazette (p. 30), Steve Miller (p. 23), Tia Owens-Powers/The Town Talk (p. 19), David J. Phillip (p. 21), Don Ryan (p. 17), Mickey Welsh/Montgomery Advertiser (p. 13); *Corbis*: ©Karen Kasmauski (p. 5); *Getty Images*: Tim Boyle (pp. 7, 23), Hulton Archive (p. 27), Richards/Fox Photos (p. 25); Michael P. Goecke (pp. 15, 29); *iStockphoto*: ©iStockphoto.com/Purdue9394 (p. 5); *Photo Researchers, Inc.*: Véronique Burger (p. 19).

Library of Congress Cataloging-in-Publication Data

Murray, Julie, 1969-
  Nurses / Julie Murray.
    p. cm. -- (Going to work. School edition)
  ISBN 978-1-61613-507-2
  1. Nurses--Juvenile literature. 2. Nursing--Juvenile literature. I. Title.
  RT61.5.M87 2011
  610.73--dc22

                                                                    2009050838

Contents

People at Work

Going to work is an important part of life. At work, people use their skills to complete tasks and earn money.

There are many different types of workplaces. Schools, factories, and offices are all workplaces.

Some nurses work in schools. They help keep schools healthy. And, they teach students about health. Their work is important to the educational success of students.

School nurses have offices inside school buildings.

A Nurse's Job

School nurses work with students of all ages. Some work at one school. Others care for students in several schools.

Nurses check in with school workers and parents. They help students who are sick or have special needs. They also find out why students are staying home sick.

Both men and women work as nurses.

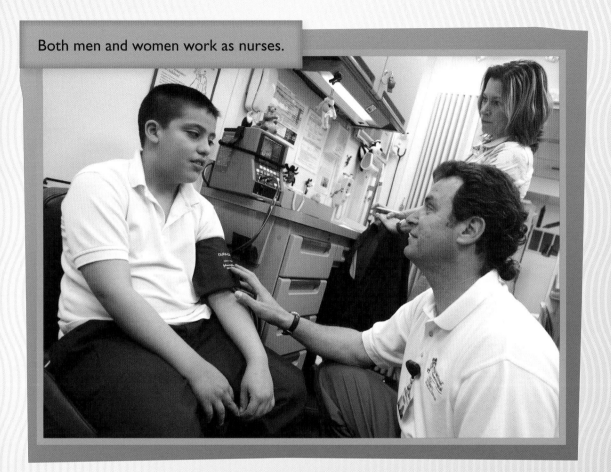

School nurses may work as a team. Sometimes. they attend meetings with other nurses in nearby schools. They talk about changes in nursing laws and how to care for students.

Did You Know?

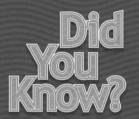

Most school nurses work full-time. They may start work before the school day and finish after it ends.

Each day is different for a school nurse. But, there are some tasks that nurses do regularly. For example, they give **medicine** to students during school.

School nurses are caring. They are concerned about each student's health.

Did You Know?

In college, students choose what they want to study, such as nursing. They take classes to learn about the subject. Then, they receive a degree in that subject.

Nursing School

To become a school nurse, a person must earn a **degree** in nursing. After completing college, he or she must pass a test to get a **license**.

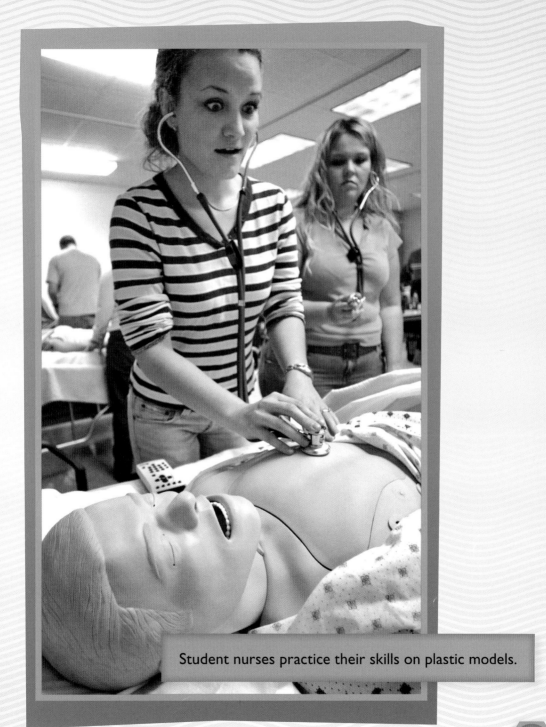

Student nurses practice their skills on plastic models.

In some states, school nurses need to earn a special **certificate**. This proves they know the most current health laws. It shows they are prepared to treat students in schools.

After they are hired, school nurses may continue to take classes. They learn about important changes and new ideas in nursing.

Nurses are good listeners. They ask questions to help students describe how they feel.

A Day at Work

School nurses use basic nursing skills to care for each student. They can check a student's temperature and heartbeat.

But, school nurses do not usually treat student illnesses. Instead, they decide if a student should stay in school. They may suggest a student see a doctor or go home.

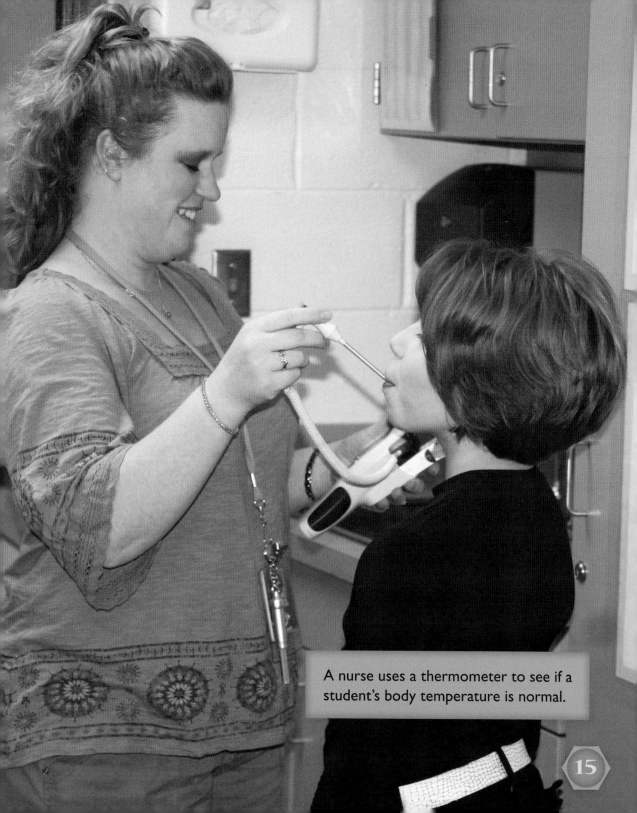

A nurse uses a thermometer to see if a student's body temperature is normal.

Working Together

School nurses are trained to care for students with special needs or health problems. They work with teachers to create learning plans for these students.

School nurses talk to students, parents, and school workers about healthy foods and exercise. They may hold health fairs to educate the community, too.

School nurses may work with students in classrooms. They teach them hand washing and other ways to care for their bodies.

17

School Work

School nurses do checkups for the whole school. These include hearing and eyesight tests.

Nurses visit classrooms to teach students about health. They talk about eating healthy foods, getting enough sleep, and staying active. They also explain the importance of brushing teeth and washing hands.

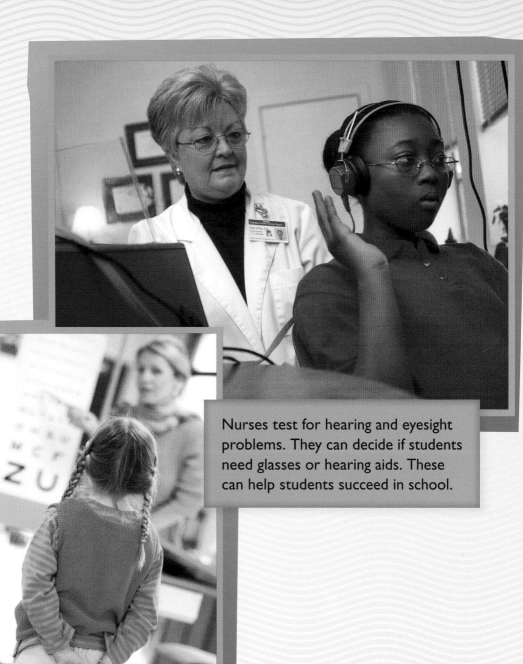

Nurses test for hearing and eyesight problems. They can decide if students need glasses or hearing aids. These can help students succeed in school.

School nurses watch the overall health of the school. Sometimes, many students and teachers become sick at the same time. Nurses let the principal and others know. Together, they take steps to prevent more illnesses.

School nurses are trained to be ready for anything. That includes **emergencies**, such as fires. In this case, nurses provide care for students and school workers.

Nurses teach students how to stay healthy. They can offer ideas for simple steps to stop illnesses from spreading.

Tools of the Trade

School nurses use special tools to do their job. They use a stethoscope to hear a student's breathing or heartbeat. And, they use an otoscope to look at a student's throat. Nurses also use computers to write notes.

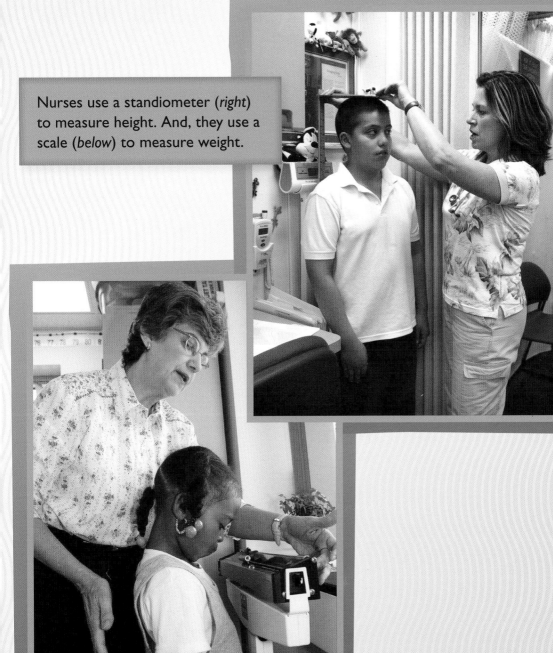

Nurses use a standiometer (*right*) to measure height. And, they use a scale (*below*) to measure weight.

HISTORY LESSON

The first school nurse was Amy Hughes. In 1892, she studied students at a school in London, England. She found that many students didn't have basic health care at home.

Then in 1898, the London School Nurses' Society formed. It brought nurses into some of London's poorest schools. The nurses treated ill students.

In 1902, Lina Rogers became the first public health school nurse in New York City, New York. She helped reduce the spread of illness. Her work allowed more students to stay in school.

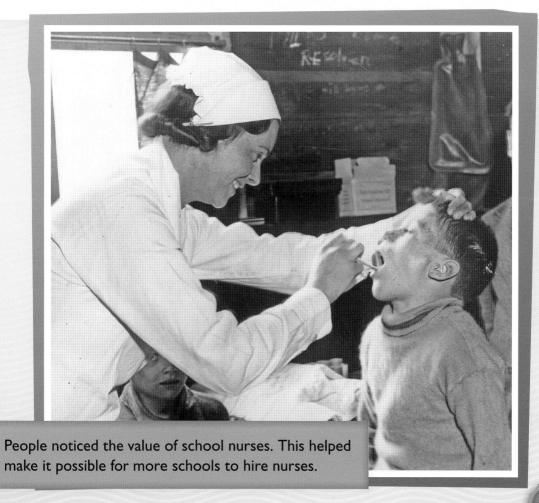

People noticed the value of school nurses. This helped make it possible for more schools to hire nurses.

For many years, caring for sick students was the main duty of school nurses. But in the 1940s, their duties increased. They began teaching students and teachers about improving health.

Over the years, school nurses helped start school health programs. They now speak in support of students and their health. Many students talk with nurses about health questions.

Long ago, school nurses used some of the same tools nurses use today.

27

Helpful Workers

School nurses do many important tasks. They work in schools to provide care for students. School nurses help students and school workers live healthy. This is meaningful work that benefits their communities!

School nurses help if students are hurt or have an emergency.

29

The School News

More Nurses Needed

According to the National Association of School Nurses, there are not enough nurses. Nursing groups and the government suggest one nurse be available for every 750 students. But sometimes, school nurses care for many more!

Is That a Fact?

Schools in Boston, Massachusetts, provided health services for students back in 1894. They were the first schools to take steps to prevent the spread of illness. School workers told ill students to stay home.

Important Words

certificate (suhr-TIH-fih-kuht) a piece of paper that proves someone has completed training.

degree a title given by a college to its students for completing their studies.

emergency (ih-MUHR-juhnt-see) an unexpected event that requires immediate action.

license (LEYE-suhnts) a paper or a card showing that someone is allowed to do something by law.

medicine (MEH-duh-suhn) an item used in or on the body to treat an illness, ease pain, or heal a wound.

Web Sites

To learn more about nurses, visit ABDO Publishing Company online. Web sites about nurses are featured on our Book Links page. These links are routinely monitored and updated to provide the most current information available.

www.abdopublishing.com

Index